SEASONS GREETINGS

FROM

TREND (IRELAND)

Dundalk & North Louth

Cuchulainn's Country

Paintings by Gerry Clarke

Text by Harold O'Sullivan

Cottage Publications

First published by Cottage Publications,
Donaghadee, N. Ireland 1997.
Copyrights Reserved.
© Illustrations by Gerry Clarke 1997.
© Text by Harold O'Sullivan 1997.
Design and origination in Northern Ireland
Printed in Singapore.

ISBN 1 900935 06 6

The Artist

Gerry Clarke is a self-taught artist who has always lived and worked in the Dundalk area. His reputation however extends worldwide with commissions going as far afield as the United States, Australia and across Europe.

As well as teaching art classes from his studio Gerry exhibits his own work regularly and is a member of the North Louth Painters Group. He is kept busy with commissions, working in various mediums and has won numerous awards. For the last eight years he has also been illustrating the cover of 'Ireland's Own' magazine

Gerry works from his home in the Kilcurry area were he lives with his wife Mary and five children.

The Author

Harold O'Sullivan is a graduate of the University of Dublin and holds the degrees of M.Litt., and Ph.D. His specialisation is seventeenth century Irish history.

An historian of the borderlands of Louth and Southeast Ulster, he has published regularly in the Louth Archaeological and Historical Journal and in Seanchas Ardhmacha, the Historical Journal of the Diocese of Armagh. He co-authored with Joseph Gavin Dundalk a Military History, (Dundalgan Press) and was co-editor with Raymond Gillespie of The Borderlands, (Institute of Irish Studies, Belfast) and also contributed "The Magennis Lordship of Iveagh in the Early Modern Period 1534-1691" in Down History and Society, (Geography Publications).

Harold and his wife Lily live in Dundalk.

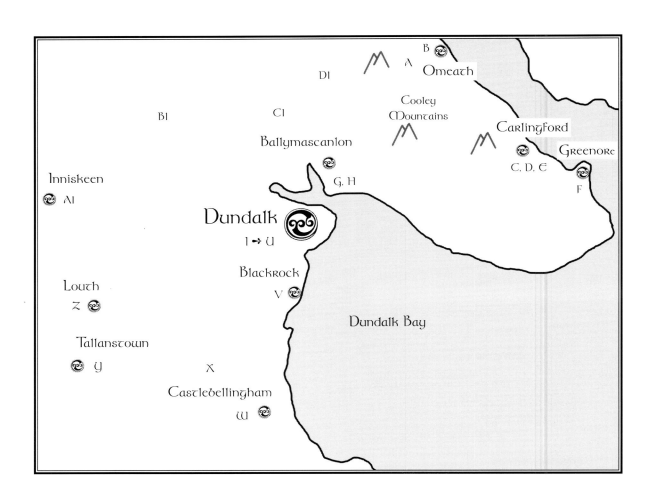

B

DI

A

B1

Cl

Cooley
Mountains

Omeath

Carlingford

Ballymascanlon

Greenore

Inniskeen

G, H

C, D, E

A1

F

Dundalk

I ➔ U

Blackrock

Louth

V

Z

Dundalk Bay

Tallanstown

Y

X

Castlebellingham

W

Contents

North Louth, Cuchulainn's Country

North Louth first emerges into history as part of the kingdom of the Connaille, an ancient people whose eponymous and mythical ancestor was Conall Cernach, friend and companion of Cuchulainn. This kingdom is described in the life of the fifth century Saint Darerca, as consisting of the territories of Muirthemne, Cúailgne and Cobha. Darerca better known as St. Monenna was baptised by St. Patrick in Cobha and later founded the convent of Killeavy in south Armagh having previously been settled on Faughart Hill north of Dundalk. The disturbance caused by a noisy wedding party held near her convent caused her to abandon the latter, and to move northwards to Killeavy. The three sub-divisions of the ancient kingdom can be readily identified. Muirthemne is the great plain, which stretches southwards along the coast from Faughart and the hills of south Armagh, to the Glyde River, which is its southern boundary. The plain also includes such inland areas as Louth, Castlering and Inniskeen. Cúailgne or Cooley is the peninsula, the north shore of which is the southern shore of Carlingford Lough and its southern boundary the north shore of Dundalk Bay. Cobha or Magh Cobha is in County Down and comprises the western areas of the county, northwards from Newry including Lurgan in County Armagh and Lisburn outside Belfast, better known today as the baronies of Upper and Lower Iveagh. The connection between Cobha and the kingdom of the Connaille is preserved to this day in the district of Clanconnell i.e., Clann Connaille, comprising the modern County Down parishes of Donacloney and Tullylish. These identifications place North Louth as part of the ancient province of Ulster comprised in one of the sub-kingdoms of the Uladh, the people who ruled over the eastern parts of the province in Antrim and Down before the coming of the Normans. This connection with Ulster has persisted to modern times, in the distinctive North Louth 'Ulster' accent; in the common history of the borderlands of south-east Ulster and in the many Irish surnames commonly met with and which have their origins in the adjacent Ulster counties of Monaghan, Armagh and Down.

Not least of the cultural bonds with Ulster is the ancient epic literature of the early Christian

Cuchulainn's Country

period known as the Ulster Cycle; the most popular of which is the Táin Bó Cúailgne or Cattle Raid of Cooley. The epic stories, which constitute this literature, relate to the period before the coming of Christianity and may have had their remote origins in the myths and legends, which the ancient Connaille of North Louth inherited from their pagan past. They were compiled, for the most part, in the monasteries of North Louth about the eight century, and in the year 835 a version of the Táin and possibly other stories, were brought by Áedacán abbot of Louth to the monastery of Clonmacnoise in County Westmeath. There they remained unnoticed for upwards of three hundred years, when another scribe with North Louth connections, Mael Muire mac Célechair mic Cuinn na mBocht, produced a second version of the epic in the twelfth century. Known as Leabhair na hUidhre or Book of the Dun Cow it survives to this day as the oldest manuscript of Irish prose tales. More than fifty percent of the place-names in the Táin are located in North Louth one of which, Delca Muirthemne or Dundalk, was the home of the mythical hero of the story, the great Cuchulainn or Hound of Ulster, thus fully justifying the description of the area as the 'Cuchulainn's Country'.

Long before Ireland ever existed, the bedrock on which the soils of North Louth were subsequently laid down was formed from layers of mud and sand sediments deposited in a deep primeval ocean some 430-408 million years ago. These layers were subsequently raised from the sea as silurian or greywhacke rock during the later Caledonian upheaval when the land was located closer to the equator and desert conditions prevailed. By the later carboniferous period of 350-300 million years ago the land had again subsided beneath the sea and in the tropical swamp conditions which then prevailed, skeletal remains of plants and shell fish accumulated on the sea floor to such a thickness that the lower layers consolidated into limestone rock with the upper layers forming sandstone and shale with later vegetable debris materials being metamorphosed into coal. These carboniferous deposits occurred throughout Ireland, but were subsequently eroded. In North Louth only in the Cooley peninsula and Faughart are deposits of carboniferous limestone to be found.

The next great change in the landscape of primeval North Louth occurred in the Tertiary period of about 65 million years ago. By this time the Irish rock structure had been virtually completed, while to the west the Atlantic Ocean has begun to take shape. To the north, Greenland had broken off from Scandanavia and began drifting westwards giving rise to immense volcanic activity which manifested itself in the Cooley peninsula and in south Armagh and which may have continued for a period of 15 million years. In this period two active volcanoes existed, one south of Slieve Gullion in Armagh and the other in Glenmore between Slieve Foy and Slieve na Glug in the Cooley peninsula. Only the eroded core of this complex now remains as ring dykes at Slieve Gullion and Slieve Foy. The latter, composed of gabbro, a hard dark coloured coarse-grained basaltic rock forms the north ring of the dyke. With the exception of Sliabh na Glug the soft moulded slopes of the southern and western ring, including Slieve na Glug and Clermont Mountain, are granophyre, possibly metamorphosed from the earlier silurian and limestone rock layers.

If the underlying rock on which North Louth rests dates from unimaginably remote times, the land surface itself is almost modern, dating from the last Ice-age of the Pleistocene Glaciation which ended a mere 10,000 years ago after a period of 2 million years of alternating glaciations. During this era alternating periods of temperate climate occurred between glaciations but only deposits from the last glaciation survive in County Louth. At the height of the glaciation, Louth was covered over by hundreds of feet of ice while the Carlingford Lough area was the terminus of a great glacier which stretched north-westwards across Armagh into Tyrone. As the ice retreated against the onset of warm conditions, the melt waters pouring into the sea, gradually raising the sea level while the land itself began to appear, covered over by deposits of clay and sand produced by the grinding action of the ice mass on the underlying rocks. In the western parts of North Louth drumlin hillocks of heavy clay are to be found, while the retreating ice left a succession of gravel ridges or eskers on the landscape several of which traverse County Louth the most important being Tullyesker at Monasterboice north of Drogheda. Perhaps the most dramatic effect of the retreating ice still to be seen in the landscape is Carlingford Lough, a natural fjord formed by the effects of the retreating glacier.

With the great weight of ice taken off the underlying land mass, a period of isostatic movements took place as the elasticity of the land mass reacted to the freedom released by the removal of the weight of the retreating ice. This was best manifested along the shoreline and which continued long after the commencement of human settlement in the area. Thus, it was that

Cuchulainn's Country

on the northern shores of Dundalk Bay the isostatic movement raised earlier beaches several feet above sea level, while on the south side of Dundalk town an eustatic change in sea levels caused by the flow of the melt-water from the retreating ice resulted in the flooding of the earlier beach including peat or bog lands which had developed in the earlier period. South of Dundalk including the valleys of the Fane and Glyde rivers a complex of sand and gravel deposits exists along with raised beaches and mud flats, the latter to be observed to this day. Land reclamations, including sea ramparts constructed in the eighteenth and nineteenth centuries in the South Marsh and Mooretown Dromiskin suggest the existence of land areas subject to flooding in relatively recent times but now protected by the sea ramparts and by the further growth of the mud flats on the southern and western shores of Dundalk Bay.

Following the immediate termination of the Ice-age the climate was warm, facilitating the rapid growth of vegetation including afforestation and with 'land bridges' still existing between Ireland and Britain and between the latter and mainland Europe many animal species made their way into the newly emerged terrain. Perhaps the most impressive of these was the Giant or Irish Elk, a skeleton of which was discovered in

Newtownbabe, Ballybarrack. Inevitably with the arrival of animal life, including fish and shellfish, human settlement followed. The earliest arrivals were of the late Mesolithic period of c3500 B.C.. These were hunter-gatherers who settled on the shore line and in some cases along river banks where primary and secondary sites have been discovered, the most important of which are in the raised beaches at Rockmarshall on the northern shore of Dundalk Bay. These have been found to be similar to those also found along the Antrim and Down coasts and at Campbeltown on the west coast of Scotland. In addition to shellfish remains, which appear to have been a substantial part of their diet, these first humans to establish themselves in North Louth also left behind artifacts of their hunting occupations such as flint implements including arrow heads.

The second phase of human settlement in North Louth known as the Neolithic or middle Stone Age of c2500 B.C., is well represented in the Castletown river valley where megalithic passage tombs existed at Killin Hill. The principal human settlements of this period were however in the upland areas, notably the Ravensdale side of Clermont Mountain and at Grange Irish near Carlingford. The attractions for settlement in the upland areas were that trees and scrub cover was less dense than in the lowlands, thus enabling clearance of the land to be effected, the soil of which was lighter than in the lowlands and therefore easier to till. In time, the conditions of the soil changed causing iron to leach and to form an impermeable layer below the surface. Allied to a possible change in climatic conditions, the land became waterlogged eventually leading to the blanket-bogs frequently met with in upland areas, examples of which are to be found at Ravensdale and Annaverna. This development led to a migration into the lowland areas where by 2000 B.C., the later Bronze Age culture had begun. The remains left behind by the earlier Neolithic farmers survive today in the megalithic tombs at Annaskeagh and Clermont Mountain, portal tombs such as the massive Proleek Dolmen at Ballymascanlon and the court-cairns of Rockmarshall, Drumnasillagh and the Commons of Carlingford. Suggesting some degree of continuity with the earlier period is the wedge-tomb near the Proleek Dolmen, which dates from the early Bronze Age. In the Cooley Mountains many barrows and cairns of the Bronze Age period are to be found, the most notable of which is perhaps the cairn on top of Carnawaddy in the townland of Doolargy, visible on the skyline above Ballymakellett.

The last of the great pre-historic ages known as the Iron Age commenced in Ireland in the second half of the last millennium B.C., and continued into the Christian era after 500 A.D.. It is to the Christian era that most of the numerous ringforts to be found in North Louth belong. An important feature of the archaeology of North Louth, dating from the early Christian era are the souterrains; underground structures of drystone walling with large stone lintels, frequently described as caves, and used as places of refuge in time of danger and perhaps also to store valuables. North Louth has one of the greatest concentrations of souterrains in Ireland, most of them located in the ancient plain of Muirthemne, the place most closely associated with that ancient people, the Connaille and to whom such diverse individuals as Conall Cernach, Cuchulainn and Darerca belonged.

S ituated at the "Windy Gap", in a cleft formed between the south-western slopes of Sliabh Foye and an eastern spur of Carnawaddy mountain called Sliabhtrasna, or the "Cross-wise Mountain" in the townland of Corrakit, the "Long Woman's Grave" is a favourite parking and picnicking area for visitors to the Cooley Mountains.

From this vantage point Glanmore or the "Big Glen" of the Sliabh Foye ring dyke can be viewed to the east with the southern section of the dyke at Sliabh na Glug visible in the distance. To the west another glen incorporating the ten townlands of Omeath, encircled by the mountains of Carnawaddy and Clermont, slope gently to the Lough shore at Narrow Water and Omeath village.

Probably the site of a destroyed gallery grave, the legend of the "Long Woman's Grave" is associated with a Lorcan O'Hanlon, one of the O'Hanlon sept of south Armagh, whose territories included the Omeath areas of North Louth down to the beginning of the sixteenth century. Lorcan ventured as far as Spain where he married a Spanish lady of noble rank. Boasting of his vast estates in Ireland he filled the lady with great expectations of her future home. Arriving at that home in the Windy Gap where she viewed only barren mountains, scattered boulders and marshy bogs, she dropped dead with disappointment. Lorcan consumed also by grief threw himself into the nearby marsh where he drowned. She, it is said, was an extraordinarily tall woman and hence her grave became known as the "Long Woman's Grave".

Unfortunately no grave, whether gallery or otherwise, has survived.

Cooley Mountains
THE LONG WOMAN'S GRAVE

With thanks to Louth County Council

The village of Omeath evolved from the railway station established there in 1876, becoming in time, a favourite resort for day-trippers from Northern Ireland and elsewhere. Unlike Warrenpoint, Omeath never developed into a major residential centre, albeit the ferry provides a close link between the two places, especially in the summer season, with local licensing laws or currency exchange rates providing additional attractions from time to time. Neither was smuggling an unknown practice among the more intrepid, especially during and after the war years.

Omeath has an ancient history. Originally Cuan Snámh Aigneach, or the "Bay of the Swim of Aigneach", the Aighneachta were the people of the Connaille who inhabited the place before the Viking settlements of the ninth and tenth centuries. Their early Christian monastery of Cillansnámh or "Church of the Swim" at Narrow Water was destroyed by the Vikings in 841 A.D.. In 928 A.D. Muirchertach Mac Neill expelled the Vikings from their settlements in the Lough which included areas such as the lands of the Aigneachta, Newry and the northern shore as far as Benna Boairche. His successor Muirchertach Mac Lochlainn later granted the lands about Newry to the newly founded Cistercian monastery in 1156, while his ally Donnchad O'Carroll, king of Airghialla got Benna Boirche and Aigneachta. The latter then settled them with Airghiallan peoples, the former with the Mugdorna from whom Mourne gets its name and the latter with the Ui Meith now Omeath.

Donnchad's son Murchadh, the last of the O'Carroll kings of Airghialla signed Mac Lochlainn's grant to the Cistercians as "King of Omeath".

Cooley Peninsula
OMEATH

With thanks to Picture Framers & Art Suppliers Ltd, Dundalk

The quay of the original harbour of Carlingford is now a small road or lane-way, which runs roughly northwest/southeast from Taaffe's castle. Many of the buildings fronting the old harbour are built gable-ended to the quay, evidently to facilitate the loading and unloading of ships. The main road outside the harbour was the line of the Newry and Greenore railway, the only remains of which now surviving is the bridge over the main road leading into King John's castle.

In the early nineteenth century Carlingford had a population of 1,110 whose principal occupations were agriculture, fishing and limestone-quarrying. The remains of the quarries can be seen on the back road to Dundalk. In addition, Wicklow and Isle of Man fishermen used Carlingford as a base to fish for herring, while the locals concentrated on the harvesting of oysters and mussels. Although the shoals of herring are long gone, the cultivation of oysters and mussels is still an important local industry with the Carlingford oyster enjoying a national reputation.

The closure of the local railways did not affect the attractions of Carlingford as a holiday centre. Since winning the National Tidy Towns competition in 1988, the local community has put in place an extensive local development scheme aimed at the preservation of the medieval character of the town while at the same time providing the visitor with all modern conveniences including hotel and guesthouse accommodation. Other facilities include an Adventure Centre, a Yacht Club and Marina, periodic festivals and cruises around Carlingford Lough in the summer season.

Carlingford
CARLINGFORD HARBOUR

With thanks to McKevitts' Village Hotel

Situated on a rocky outcrop, immediately above the harbour, King John's Castle is an early thirteenth century construction the order for the building of which is attributed to King John on the occasion of his visit to Carlingford in 1210. It has a "D" shaped courtyard facing south-west with the remains of the entrance gate immediately north of the modern entrance, the walling of which may pre-date the king's visit. The inner two-storey building or Hall may have been a remodelling of the castle carried out c1261 while parts of the south-eastern corner towards the cliff edge is a reconstruction of the fifteenth/sixteenth centuries.

The damaged section of the castle in this area is probably the result of a "slighting" of the castle by the Cromwellian commander Colonel Venables when, after the storming of Drogheda in 1649, he was dispatched northwards to capture Dundalk and Carlingford. The arrival of Venables' forces south of the town coincided with the arrival of a man-of-war, with provisions and a battery of cannon, which was greeted by a few hostile shots from the castle as she passed by. Before Venables could attack the castle the garrison, probably with Drogheda in mind, surrendered under articles and marched away to Newry.

The nearby Taaffe's Castle, which stood in the old harbour area of the town, is a large fifteenth-sixteenth century tower house. Its name may derive from Theobald Taaffe, earl of Carlingford, who acquired extensive properties in and around Carlingford during the seventeenth century restoration land settlement.

Carlingford
KING JOHN'S CASTLE

With thanks to The Oyster Catcher, Carlingford

Although frequently attributed to the Vikings, the foundation of Carlingford was the work of the Norman baron Hugh de Lacy in the late twelfth or early thirteenth centuries. The infant town was captured by King John in 1210 in pursuit of the delinquent de Lacy who had "gone on his keeping" across the Lough into County Down. About this time, was commenced the great stone castle known as King John's Castle on the western approaches to the town.

Throughout the Middle Ages Carlingford was a defensive bastion for the old English colony in Cooley and Carlingford as well as providing a trading and market centre for the area, where de Lacy had a grant of a fair as early as 1227. In the early fourteenth century Richard de Burgo earl of Ulster bought out the de Lacy interests and founded the Dominican Priory in 1305, the ruins of which still survive.

Carlingford prospered throughout the sixteenth and seventeenth centuries, mainly from war-related trade into south-east Ulster where men and cargo had to be transhipped in smaller vessels for the trip up the Lough into Newry. With the construction of the Newry Ship Canal in the early eighteenth century, enabling ships to by-pass the port, Carlingford went into decline. A modern benefit of this has been the preservation of the medieval character of the place which is now one of the Heritage towns of Ireland. With the coming of the railways the town evolved as a popular tourism resort and so remains to this day.

Carlingford

GHAN COTTAGE AND THE THOLSEL

With thanks to Tholsel Crafts

In a county noted for its antiquities it comes as something of a shock to discover that the history of Greenore commenced only in the last century. A creature of the burgeoning railway industry of the period, its development was the result of collaboration in the 1860's, between the Dundalk and Enniskillen and the London and North-Western Railway Companies.

The port of Greenore possesses two important attributes, firstly its sheltered location and secondly, its deep water, enabling ships to be worked at all stages of the tides. Realising the advantages of opening up a sea route connecting the southern and western regions of Ulster with England, facilitating travel (including tourism) between the two countries, it was decided to service the port by two railway systems, one from Greenore to Dundalk and the other from Greenore to Newry.

Financial and other difficulties soon beset the adventure, and it was not until April 1873 that the port became operational through the Greenore to Dundalk section of the railway-line. The Greenore to Newry section was completed in 1876 and thereafter the railway became known as the Dundalk, Newry and Greenore Railway Company.

The L.N.W. Railway Company was responsible for the development of the port and its facilities including a hotel, several housing schemes, a school and a golf course.

While the tourism legacy still remains, the railways have all gone, victims of the railway "rationalisation" schemes of the early 1950's. Greenore village was subsequently sold off and the port acquired by private interests.

Greenore
The Quays at Greenore

With thanks to the Fairways Hotel & Leisure Centre

Proleek Dolmen is situated north of the Ballymascanlon House Hotel and is accessible via a concrete bridge over the Flurry river on the Proleek roadway leading north from Ballymascanlon Bridge. Proleek meaning a stone burial place, obviously takes its name from the dolmen which is a portal tomb, one of four in the county, all of which are located in the countryside north of Dundalk. It belongs to the Neolithic period of c2500 B.C..

A particular feature of the dolmen is the huge size of the capstone estimated to be fifty tons in weight standing on relatively slender and tall support stones, a remarkable balancing act that has stood the test of time. It is speculated that the capstone, which is an igneous dolerite rock of the type found in the boulder clay west and south east of Sliabh Gullion, was pulled into position on wooden rollers on a gradually sloping ramp, but how the subsequent balancing act was achieved remains a mystery.

When completed the whole structure would have been enclosed in a cairn of stone and earth, long since eroded. Archeological experience indicates that it was a site for cremated burials. Local tradition avers that those with matrimonial intentions in mind can have their ambitions realised within one year by successfully landing one stone in three on the top of the capstone, the achievement of which is not impossible.

Close by is a Bronze Age wedge tomb or gallery grave c2000 B.C., and classified as a "Cist Burial".

Ballymascanlon

PROLEEK DOLMEN

With thanks to The Lisdoo Arms

This much photographed and painted group of estate cottages situated on the Dundalk to Carlingford road at Ballymascanlon bridge formerly belonged to the Plunketts, the last of whom Katherine, daughter of the second baron Plunkett, died in 1932 aged 112 years. She lies buried in Ballymascanlon graveyard. The House is now the nearby Ballymascanlon House Hotel.

Ballymascanlon is a village settlement of considerable antiquity, probably taking its name from Scanlan chief of the Ui Meith who died in 672 A.D.. In 833, a Mac Scanlon repulsed a raid by the Danes in the Dundalk Bay area. After the Norman settlement the district was granted by Hugh de Lacy to Mellifont Abbey and in time became known as the Lordship of Ballymascanlon, or more commonly as Lordship. On the south side of the village beside the river lies a ruined watermill, the site of which may date from the thirteenth century.

After the dissolution of the monasteries, Lordship passed to the Moore family. Sir Garrett Moore was a friend of Hugh O'Neill earl of Tyrone, who appears to have leased Ballymascanlon to him in the 1580's-1590's when O'Neill occupied a tower house in the area. The Church of Ireland parish church is located south of the roadway and within a few hundred yards of the village. Almost certainly this was the site of the medieval church, reported in 1622 as "repaired". A small building close by the present church may have been an eighteenth century presbyterian meeting-house, the history of which is obscure.

Ballymascanlon

BALLYMASCANLON COTTAGES

With thanks to Mr Jim O Callaghan, TSM Control Systems

Tradition has it that the original "Big Bridge" was a multi-arched structure, which was replaced by the present three-arched bridge in 1819. The existing structure was indeed built in 1819 by the County Louth Grand Jury at a cost of about £5,000, replacing an earlier bridge, but which was also three-arched. A map of c1770 shows the latter on the existing site, suggesting that the present bridge may have been erected on its foundations.

Originally there was a ford across the river at this place identified in the Táin Bó Cúailgne as Áth Carpat or "Ford of the Chariots", but by 1418 a bridge had been constructed, to which a Matthew Fleming of Dundalk left a legacy of 2 marks. It is possible that this was the original Big Bridge.

The bridge is a good vantage point to view the surrounding countryside. To the west the original Dún Dealgan can be viewed, tree shrouded on top of the ridge at Castletown. Due west is tree-covered Killen Hill legendary burial-place of Cian mac Cainte of the ancient tale of the Children of Turenn. To the north-west can be seen the hills at Forkhill in south Armagh including Crosslieve, Tievecrom and Carrickbroad forming the southern parts of the Sliabh Gullion ring dyke. To the north-east lies the Cooley mountain range sloping down to Dundalk Bay.

The immediate vicinity, north of the bridge, was the site of Schomberg's fatal encampment of 1689 where hundreds of his troops died of disease.

Dundalk

THE BIG BRIDGE

With thanks to P. B. Gunne Auctioneers

This is the place referred to in the Táin Bó Cúailgne as Delca Muirthemne and recognised in other stories of the Ulster Cycle as the home and last resting place of the hero Cuchulainn and his wife Emer. In its existing condition it is the remains of a late twelfth century Norman motte and bailey, the building of which is ascribed to Bertram de Verdon c1190. Delca, later Dún Dealgan may translate as Brooch, i.e., the Brooch of Muirthemne or Thorn, the Thorn Fort. The latter would suggest that the site was formerly a raised fort of the early Christian period and subsequently re-fashioned into a motte and bailey by the de Verdons.

Despite its venerable history the Mount has not experienced the respect which it deserved from succeeding generations. It seems to have been abandoned after the completion of Roche Castle in the thirteenth century and the site occupied by native Irish, which would account for the souterrain set into the southern side of the motte.

In 1780, a local merchant and shipper named Patrick Byrne, whose pseudonym "the Pirate", suggests that not all his trafficking was above board, built a substantial mansion-house, or folly, on top of the motte with an avenue from the roadway through the bailey and circling the motte to the top. The house survived to 1923, when it was burned down during the Civil War. Further encroachment of the site took place in recent times when the bailey was substantially destroyed in the construction of the waterworks.

Dundalk
CASTLETOWN MOUNT

With thanks to P. Lavelle & Sons

T his, the most venerable of the churches of Dundalk, dates from the very foundation of the town in the thirteenth century, the graveyard of which is mentioned in a deed dated 1325.

Cruciform in design with nave, transepts and polygonal chancel, it is an early eighteenth century remodelling of the earlier church devastated in the Jacobite/Williamite Wars. Elements of the earlier period can still be identified including an arcaded south wall, and a tall three-stage church tower with a buttress-like projection on the southwestern corner which houses a spiral staircase. The green copper spire on top of the tower is a replacement of an earlier spire designed by Francis Johnston in 1786, and from which its description as the Green Church is derived.

Recently repaired and refurbished, the interior still retains its eighteenth century character. In 1812, the triple-light east window was embellished by a mosaic of renaissance style glass of Flemish origins, donated to the church by the earl of Roden. One of the pieces contains a picture representing two bishops with a Latin inscription commemorating the death in 1373, of Saint Andrew, bishop of Fiestole, 'by birth of the noble family of the Corsini'.

Burials in the churchyard include the medieval primate Richard Fitzralph, better known throughout the Middle Ages as Saint Richard of Dundalk, whose modern chapel is in the southern transept, and Agnes Gault sister of the Scots poet, Robbie Burns, whose grave is marked by a pillar stone to the right of the entrance gate.

Dundalk

ST. NICHOLAS'S, C. OF I. PARISH CHURCH

With thanks to R. Q. O'Neill

Clanbrassil Street and Church Street date from the very beginnings of the town in the thirteenth century.

Vestiges of Lord Limerick's re-developments of the 1740's have survived within the Victorian façades of the nineteenth century, providing a unique character to these, the principal streets of the town. Among the most important of these are No.63, a stuccoed Italianate building constructed in 1870 with panelled pilasters, elaborate window surrounds, rosettes and keystones bearing bearded heads. No.70, constructed in 1868 as a wine store, has four giant arches standing above the ground floor and framing the upper stories of the façade topped by a balustrade, with keystones and diamond shaped reliefs between each storey.

Across the street is Deary's Department Store with very fine curved glass display windows, plinths, corner quoin pilasters and ball finials of pink and grey polished granite. This has been one of the leading drapery establishments of the town since its foundation in 1834. Other buildings of note include the Clanbrassil Hotel, McEvoy's Department Store and the A.I.B. Bank.

Church Street, which takes its name from the Green Church, was the town centre until the eighteenth century re-developments. A market square stood between the Church and Mr. Cashell's house (now the site of Dundalk House built in 1911).

The Guildhall and Tholsel occupied the street south of the Church and opposite the former Carroll's Wholesale Offices. The latter being an Edwardian building dating from 1910, its central entrance has a large segmental pediment flanked by segmented-headed windows and pretty neo-rococo cast-iron grilles.

Dundalk
CLANBRASSIL STREET

With thanks to R. Q. O'Neill

Described by Sir Walter Scott in 1825 as "a magnificent Justice Hall, a public building superior, I think, to any in Edinburgh", Dundalk Courthouse was built between 1813 and 1818, the portico of which is its principal feature.

The original specification required that the portico be designed according to "the patterns and true proportions of the rules of Grecian architecture as they are to be collected from the ruins of the city of Athens" and, not "those of the common books of architecture of ordinary use and application in this country". Built by the County Louth Grand Jury, the design selected was that of the temple of Thesius in Athens.

Two Dublin architects, Edward Park and John Bowden, were responsible for the work, but considerable influence was brought to bear by two of the Grand-jurors, John Leslie Foster of Collon and Blaney Townley Balfour of Townley Hall. It appears that their contribution was the two massive columns standing within the portico, which draws the latter into the inner hall, but which was not provided for in the original design, giving rise to subsequent controversy. In a disagreement between Foster and Park, the latter was removed from the work which was completed by Bowden. William Moore, the contractor, later sued the Grand Jury for the additional costs and was awarded £12,000 compensation. As this sum could not be levied as a cess by the Grand Jury the latter found it necessary to procure a private Act of Parliament for the purpose.

Dundalk
DUNDALK COURTHOUSE

With thanks to McEvoys Department Stores

The Town Hall is the headquarters of the Dundalk Urban District Council, the successor of the Dundalk Town Commissioners and Dundalk Corporation. Since its establishment, the Council has been the housing, sanitary and roads authority for Dundalk which is the next largest town in the Republic of Ireland after Galway.

The expansion of the town in the period since independence has been due, in large measure, to the development policies of the Council. These include the provision of housing schemes; sites for private housing and industrial developments; the extension of the road network and piped water supply. A major re-vamp of the town sewerage system is currently in hand. The Council also provides a Municipal Theatre at the Town Hall, an Arts Centre, a Civic Museum, a Sports Centre and a Fire Service.

The Town Hall was originally intended as a Corn Exchange, but before it was completed the company went into liquidation. It was then taken over by a second company, and when completed in 1864 was sold to the Dundalk Town Commission. The architect was a Mr John Murray. The building included a concert hall, which was destroyed by fire in 1946, and was replaced by the present Municipal Theatre.

The Town Hall is a substantial building in brick with an Italianate façade with quoined pilasters at the ends and centre, with granite trim. It has a seven-bay frontage, with a central porch and two Ionic columns, and rustication on the ground floor.

Dundalk

DUNDALK TOWN HALL

With thanks to Dundalk Urban District Council

Better known to the people of Dundalk as the Cathedral, Saint Patrick's was built between the years 1837 and 1847 but opened for worship in 1842. It is the successor of the old Chapel in Chapel Street. It was erected under the supervision of a committee of the leading Catholic merchants and traders of the town in the immediate post-emancipation era, when at last Roman Catholics could erect their places of worship without inhibitions or prohibitions by the State. It was therefore an ambitious project intended as an expression of the growing self-confidence of the local Roman Catholic community of the time.

The architect was John Duff of Newry, who determined that the new church should be of the Gothic Perpendicular style and used as his models, King's College Chapel in Cambridge and Bath Abbey in Somerset. The belfry clock tower was erected in 1903 in the same architectural style.

This exceptionally fine church is over 1,500 feet long and accommodates up to 1,500 people. The body of the church is a long nine-bay hall of coursed granite, crenellated parapet and octagonal corner turrets. Pinnacled buttresses divide each bay with single large windows in each gable. The interior is at once elegant in appearance and simple in design, with the nave joining without interruption a two-bay chancel with arches into side chapels. The ceiling is a simple quadripartite vault with foliated bosses and angel corbel stops, all in plaster.

Dundalk

St. Patrick's Roman Catholic Church

With thanks to R. Q. O'Neill

The Louth County Library Service has its origins in the Dundalk Free Library established by the Town Commissioners in 1856 under the Public Libraries Act 1853. It was the first such library to be established in Ireland, and was the achievement of the cross-community activities of four men, the Young Irelander Patrick Comerford, Protestant Vicar of Dundalk the Rev. Elias Thackeray, medical doctor and Englishman John Browne, and County Louth member of the United Parliament Chichester Fortesque, who was responsible for the adoption of the Libraries Act 1853 in Ireland. These had been involved in the provision of free libraries and reading rooms in the town in the 1840's and 1850's and subsequently provided the newly established Free Library with a foundation book-stock of over 2,000 books.

In 1877, the Town Clerk of Dublin Corporation, in a report to the City Council, stated that Dundalk was "the only place in Ireland in which a library had been established under the Act". Although responsibility for the discharge of public library services was devolved on County Councils in 1925, this arrangement was not implemented in County Louth until 1934. In recent years the Louth County Council acquired the former early nineteenth century distillery premises on the Ramparts and, at considerable expense converted it into the headquarters of the County Library Services and Dundalk Public Library. The Reference Section includes many rare books, the legacy of Messrs., Browne, Comerford, Fortesque and Thackeray.

Dundalk
LOUTH COUNTY LIBRARY

With thanks to Ardmac Group Ltd

The Garda Siochana were established in Dundalk in 1923 in succession to the Royal Irish Constabulary, taking possession of the stations formerly occupied by the latter in Bridge Street and Anne Street and from the beginning was an unarmed police force.

In the post-war period it was decided to establish a central police station for the town and to this end the administrative wing of the former Dundalk Gaol was converted to this purpose in 1946. The gaol had been constructed in 1853, on what was formerly known as the Gallows Hill, at the junction of the Ardee and Carrickmacross roads. The architect was John Neville, then the surveyor to the County Louth Grand Jury. The building is Italianate in style and was constructed above a sloping semi-circular green frontage enclosed by a low wall. It is a rectangular two-storey structure over a concealed basement. A deep band of vermiculated rustication is at the base with projecting corner blocks and low wide-hipped roofs built of granite ashlar. The windows are square-headed on the ground floor and round-headed above. In the principal five-bay elevation, the three centre bays are recessed, screened by a tall single loggia and crowned by a two-storey tower with a pyramidal roof. Flanking the building on each side are rubble walls with cut-stone arches giving access to the rear and providing a screen above, where the quoined chimneys of the accommodation blocks of the former Gaol can be seen.

Dundalk
GARDA STATION

With thanks to Ian Carroll

The brewing industry in Dundalk dates from the Middle Ages, supplying the needs of the many taverns and 'drinking shops' in the town and county, without discrimination whether they were Gael or Gall, a practice which has continued to the present day.

In the seventeenth century there were at least six licensed breweries in the town, a trade that was continued into the eighteenth century when George Byrne had a major brewery concern in Seatown. He was not without competition; in 1779 a William Gawley was advertising cut-price beer at twenty-three shillings a barrel. Towards the end of the century James McAllister established a brewery in a former cambric factory at Casangarve on the Ardee road.

Father Matthew's crusade against intoxicating drink must have had a bad effect on the local brewing trade. By 1846 only the Cambrickville brewery and another at Dublin Street were 'doing little more than supplying local needs'. A decade later, only the Dublin Street brewery was in operation, with an output of about three hundred barrels per week. This was a partnership between the brothers John and Arthur Duffy and a Mr. E.H. Macardle. The latter acquired the interests of the former in 1863, and in partnership with Mr. A.T. Moore of Dublin, continued at Dublin Street but later transferred to Cambrickville where, as Macardle Moore & Co., it has prospered to this day.

In addition to the brewing of Macardles, the indigenous ale of North Louth, the brewery also engages in the bottling and canning of stout and other products of the Guinness range.

Dundalk

THE MACARDLE MOORE BREWERY

With thanks to the Guinness Ireland Group Ltd

Situated at the corner of Mill Street and Castle Road this "castle" is all that now remains of the Franciscan friary, founded in 1240, which was looted and destroyed by the lord deputy Gray in 1538. This was a service it also experienced at the hands of Edward Bruce in 1315 when the friary was burned down and the entire community killed.

The "castle" is the former bell tower of the friary and formed part of the friary church, the choir of which extended eastwards into Mill Street while the Nave separated by the tower, extended westwards across Castle Road. The friary buildings extended on the southern side of the church, much of the land of which is now incorporated in the Sisters of Mercy convent nearby. It had a corn-mill, an orchard and a private fish weir on the Castletown river. The friars also brewed their own beer.

After the destruction of their friary by Gray, the community continued to live in the town until they were expelled in 1563. They returned about 1626 and having established themselves as a community they opened a grammar school in the town in the following year. Despite subsequent periods of persecution, they continued to retain their connection with the town until the end of the eighteenth century. A long list of the former seventeenth and eighteenth century Guardians has survived, the last of whom was a Father Antony McMahon who signed an attestation as the actual Guardian of Dundalk in 1773.

Dundalk
SEATOWN CASTLE

With thanks to AIB Bank, Dundalk

The harbour improvements of the 1840's paved the way for a rapid expansion of activity through Dundalk port. A number of steampacket companies had established themselves by the middle of the century, including the St. George Steampacket Company of Liverpool, still commemorated in the port by St. George's Quay. A second and local company established in 1837 which operated originally from the Point, transferred to what is now the Steampacket Quay and had a small fleet of ships including paddle-steamers trading in passenger and freight through the port to Liverpool.

Throughout the famine years many hundreds of people took the emigration route through the port to Liverpool and beyond and even as late as 1857 the County Louth philanthropist Vere Foster led a party of one hundred and fifty people in an assisted passage to the United States of America. Competition entered the field in 1850 with the establishment of the Dundalk and Midlands Steamship Company by local businessman Mr. Peter Russell, who, by enclosing the sloblands at St.Helena, established Russell's, later George's and now the Railway Quay west of the harbour.

The harbour has had a chequered existence since those early entrepreneurial days as much through cut-throat competition between shipping companies and changes in trading conditions as through the constant necessity for dredging. Notwithstanding the ups and downs, the port has survived and its future is by no means dim. At present four ships are registered in Dundalk, the Rockfleet, the Rockisland, the Rockabill and the Sea Boyne.

Dundalk

DUNDALK HARBOUR

With thanks to Bord Na Móna

The first mention of a windmill in Dundalk was in 1340 when William Dowdall and Nicholas Chepman leased a plot from the Corporation "for building a windmill on the Markethill", a place which can be identified as close to present day John's Street. Although the "windmills on the seashore" mentioned in Duke's Plott were located in the Seatown-Point road area, the windmill ruin in Seatown Place was erected by a merchant named Martin in 1805, during the boom years of the Napoleonic Wars. It is seven storeys high and contained five pairs of stones, to grind fine flour, oatmeal and Indian corn. It was said to have been the largest of its kind in Ireland. The site on which it stands was formerly a brewery, owned by George Byrne, one of the leading benefactors of the mid-eighteenth century Catholic Chapel in Chapel Street. The buildings surrounding the windmill may have been part of the former brewery.

The windmill enterprise never prospered, probably because of the competition from the nearby water-mill in Mill Street the mill stream of which passes the windmill along Quay Street. It was closed by 1855 and in 1870 the sails and wooden gallery surround at the base of the windmill were taken down.

The nearby former O'Rourke's Mills, which drew its water power from the Ramparts river, had been a mill site since the late sixteenth century and was frequently referred to in eighteenth century title deeds as the 'Mill of Dundalk', where tenants of the landlord were compelled to take their corn for grinding.

Dundalk

THE WINDMILL

With thanks to Fyffes

Blackrock, in the townland of Haggardstown, is a residential area of relatively recent origins built around a nineteenth century seaside resort which itself was built around an earlier fishing village situated on the northern shores of the Fane estuary. Three miles south of Dundalk, facing eastwards into a wide bay, the Blackrock promenade provides excellent opportunities for viewing the Cooley mountain range on the north side of the bay with a similar view of distant Dunany Head on the south. The spidery looking construction on the north-eastern offshore is a lighthouse guarding the entrance to Dundalk harbour, now no longer manned.

Blackrock is a popular resort for the people of Dundalk, especially for young children learning to swim in its absolutely safe waters. It was, at an earlier period, a resort where many families from the nearby counties of Meath, Monaghan and Armagh used to come to spend holidays before the warmer climes of southern Europe tempted them away. Notwithstanding the changed times, Blackrock still draws the crowd on the fifteenth of August, the principal day in the village calendar, while the guest-houses can still attract visitors at all times of the year.

The expansion of the residential areas to the west has now engulfed both the old Irish settlement of Aschacmnacharan(Stamnacharan) with which the earthworks of Knockshee at the rear of the Fairways Hotel may be associated as well as the old English settlement of Haggardstown with its ruined churchyard. It was here that Oliver Plunkett, the saintly archbishop of Armagh, ordained priests during his ministry in Armagh.

Blackrock
The Shore at Blackrock

With thanks to Connolly's Delicatessan

Formerly Gernonstown, Castlebellingham as a place-name is derived from a Captain Henry Bellingham who got a grant of the estate of Patrick Gernon in the period of the English Commonwealth, Gernon being transplanted to Connacht. The Gernons descend from a 'long tailed' Old English kin-group, settled since the thirteenth century along the Glyde and Dee Rivers, the individual members of which had estates in Dunany, Gernonstown, Stabannon, Milltown, Killencoole, Dunmahon and Dunbin. Surviving Gernon castles are to be found at Milltown, Killencoole and Dunmahon.

Henry Bellingham's son Thomas was aide-de-camp to William of Orange whose guide he was at the battle of the Boyne. Castlebellingham also had connections with James Napper Tandy of 1798 fame who, having been accused of taking the Defenders Oath under a tree in the village in 1793, was outlawed and had to flee the country.

Although of late seventeenth century origins, Castlebellingham is the outcome of the improving efforts of the Bellingham family throughout the late eighteenth and nineteenth centuries. Although burdened by the weight of passing traffic, soon to be lifted when the new motorway is completed, Castlebellingam is an attractive and charming village worthy to stop in and to explore.

Castlebellingham Castle, located on the banks of the river Glyde is now a hotel, while the widows' almshouses built between 1826-30, situated on the driveway behind the wayside Crucifix, designed by Mr. William Vitruvius

Morrison are an important architectural feature. At the north end of the village stands a Celtic Cross, memorial to local men who died in the Great War of 1914-18.

Castlebellingham

WIDOWS' ALMSHOUSES

With thanks to Frances' Studio Ltd

The tower houses of County Louth date mainly from the fiftheenth and sixteenth centuries and while their defensive characteristics are obvious, it must also be borne in mind that, as the residences of the local landed gentry, they were also intended to impress the neighbours.

Milltown Castle belonged to a lawyer branch of the Gernons who suffered confiscation of their lands during the English Commonwealth, but recovered them in the Restoration period. Nicholas Gernon the proprietor in 1688 was killed in action against the Williamites in 1689 and his estate was subsequently forfeited. His only daughter and heir Margaret had eloped in 1681 with a William Fortesque, son of a local Protestant and was promptly disinherited by her father.

In 1694 a Mrs. Anne Baker sought a grant of the Gernon estate to herself and her children. Her claim was based on the distinguished service rendered by her late husband, Colonel Henry Baker who was joint governor of the city of Derry during the celebrated siege and where he met his death. Baker was from Dunmahon and had been a lieutenant in Newcomen's regiment of foot in Drogheda.

In subsequent legal proceedings William Fortesque succeeded in his claim thanks to the entailed nature of the estate which had descended to Edward Gernon, descendant of Patrick Gernon of Gernonstown. Being without heir he relinquished his claim in favour of Margaret, so that the estate 'should return to its own antient chanell'. Her gravestone in Dromiskin churchyard still survives.

Milltown

Milltown Castle

With thanks to Faulkner's, Castlebellingham

Tallanstown, like Castlebellingham, is a former estate village, which evolved in association with nearby Louth Hall, the former residence of the Plunketts, lords of Louth.

The Plunketts are another 'long tailed' Old English kin group who appear to have been originally settled at Beaulieu outside Drogheda, later spreading as separate families throughout Meath and Louth. The Plunketts would appear to have been settled at Tallanstown from at least the sixteenth century, holding extensive estates in Louth, Monaghan, Meath and Kildare, much of it former monastic properties acquired following the dissolution of the monasteries. Oliver the sixth baron suffered confiscation of his estates during the period of the English Commonwealth, much of which was recovered in the Restoration period by his son and heir Matthew who bought out the Commonwealth planter's interests in Tallanstown for £400 in 1661. He then re-furbished and extended the ancestral tower house, now built into Louth Hall, which was extensively rebuilt in the eighteenth century, although now much dilapidated.

Tallanstown village was built around an open triangle and is mainly early nineteenth century construction, consisting of rows of cottages to house workers employed on the nearby Lord Louth's estate. Their steep slated roofs and large redbrick chimneys are attractive features of their construction. The house on the north-western corner of the village was the manor Court; the franchises of which are no longer exercised. On the north side of the village and across the bridge there is another row of cottages built in 1851 for the tenants of Rathbrist.

Tallanstown is a prize-winner of the National Tidy Towns contest.

Tallanstown

TALLANSTOWN VILLAGE

With thanks to Pat & Sheila Smyth, Centra

In the medieval and middle age periods Louth was one of the most important centres in the county to which it later gave its name, being in pagan times a centre for the worship of Lugh, one of the principal gods of the ancient Celts.

From the beginnings of his mission in Ireland, Patrick gave close attention to Louth where he settled his disciple Mochta on the former pagan foundation of Lugh. Mochta's monastery of Louth prospered throughout the succeeding centuries until the anarchy introduced in the ninth and tenth centuries when it was regularly plundered by native Irish and Vikings alike, even to the twelfth century when all of the present day county of Louth was annexed by Donnchad O'Carroll king of the Airghialla. Due to his influence he succeeded in the separation of Louth from the diocese of Armagh and its incorporation into Clogher, the diocesan centre of which was moved to Louth.

In 1148, O'Carroll founded the Augustinian abbey of St. Mary's in association with O'Kelly, bishop of Louth, who adopted it as his cathedral and diocesan chapter. It survived as such into the early thirteenth century when Norman influence brought it back under the jurisdiction of Armagh. The only remnant of the former importance of Louth now remains in the tenth/eleventh century "Mochta's House", a stone built oratory with a probable sleeping chamber in its high vaulted roof. The remnants of St. Mary's Abbey close by is probably of fourteenth century construction, while the Norman motte castle constructed before 1196 was visited by King John in 1210.

Louth
MOCHTA'S HOUSE & ST. MARY'S ABBEY

With thanks to Finnegans Louth Post Office

The village of Inniskeen stands on the borders of Louth and Monaghan and while officially in the latter its postal address is Dundalk.

Historically part of Magh Muirthemne, it is the site of a sixth century church founded by Dáig Mac Carell. While only the Round Tower of this ancient foundation remains, its surviving historical records include a Flann O Dachua died 784 and other abbots until 930. Lactnan was coarb in 1022 and Mac Soillig erenagh in 1085.

That the Normans penetrated to Inniskeen is testified by the presence of a Norman motte and bailey located in the centre of the village.

Inniskeen is celebrated as the birthplace in 1905 of the Irish poet and playwright Paddy Kavanagh. Kavanagh is a modern expression of a literary tradition which has existed in the borderlands of south-east Ulster and North Louth since the anonymous authors of the Ulster Cycle of stories, and include more recent poets of the seventeenth to the twentieth centuries such as Peadar O'Doirnin, Art McCooey, Seamus Dall McCuartha, the late Jim Craven and still with us Conor O'Callaghan.

Paddy Kavanagh died in 1967 and was buried in the churchyard of the former Catholic parish church now the Patrick Kavanagh Rural and Literary Resource Centre, providing a focus for one of the most important, if neglected, centres of literature and poetry in Ireland.

Inniskeen is a pleasant village for a visit and has many local amenities including river walks, a pitch and putt course and a play area for children.

Inniskeen

INNISKEEN VILLAGE

With thanks to Tim & Nuala Devlin, McNellos Bar & Lounge, Inniskeen

Roche Castle stands on the Louth-Armagh borders and is accessible from the Dundalk-Armagh road south of the Drumbilla crossroads. Anciently Castellum de Rupe or Castle of the Rock, an apt name considering that it stands on the southern edge of a large rock, with its tall towers and battlemented walls visible for miles around.

It is said to have been built by Bertram de Verdon's granddaughter Rohesia sometime before 1236. Tradition has it that when it was completed Rohesia had the architect thrown from one of the windows in the northern tower, not in a dispute over his account, but to preserve the secrets of the design of the castle. As the existing ruins appear to be from a later date it is more likely that while Rohesia may have commenced its construction, its completion may have taken place in the lifetime of her son John who died in 1274.

This great castle-keep, which is comparable with castles at Carlingford and Carrickfergus in County Antrim, consists of a curtain wall enclosing a sub-triangular area with the living accommodation or hall situated on the southern side and to the left of the gateway entrance on the east wall. The gateway consists of massive twin towers, semicircular to the front and entered by a causeway across a fosse. The flat area outside the gate may have been the site of a ville or township. It survived as a defended place to the mid-seventeenth century when it was "slighted" or made ruinous by the forces of the English Commonwealth.

Roche

ROCHE CASTLE

With thanks to Trend, Distributors of Cuchulainn Crystal

The hill of Faughart is probably the most historic of the hills surrounding the town of Dundalk, showing evidence of human occupation from at least the early Christian period. Such an early date is indicated by a large double-ditched enclosure, visible only by aerial photography, which surrounds the site and which may be pre-Christian in origins.

Faughart was one of the places where Cuchulainn fought in single combat against one of Maeve's warriors, Fer Baeth, whom he killed by throwing a holly-shoot back over his shoulder striking Fer Baeth on the nape of the neck. Whence the name "Focherd" or 'good cast', later "Focherd Muirthemne".

Placed just south of the Moiry Pass and along the ancient roadway into Ulster the Slige Midlúachra, also mentioned in the Táin, Faughart is an ideal place to view the surrounding countryside of Magh Muirthemne. Because of its strategic location it is not surprising that Faughart has been the scene of many battles, in one of which fought in 672 A.D., Aedh Roin king of the Uladh was slain and his head cut off on the "Stone of Decapitation". The latter still lies near the doorway of the old church. Faughart was the meeting place between the earl of Ormond and Hugh O'Neill in 1594 and the jumping off point for Mountjoy's army into Ulster in 1600. Along with the ruins of the medieval church, there is a well, dedicated to St. Brigid and a possible early cross-site. Nearby to the west lies the ubiquitous Norman motte castle.

Faughart
HILL OF FAUGHART

With thanks to Four Counties Oil

Feede hill forms the western flank of the picturesque Ravensdale valley in County Louth as well as the eastern flank of the Moiry Pass, north of the hill of Faughart, in County Armagh where an ancient pillar stone at Kilnasaggart marks the site of an early Christian monastic settlement. The stone is carved with a cerca seventh century inscription recording that the settlement was founded by Ternoc mac Ciaran under the protection of the Apostle Peter.

Feede, which stands at an elevation of 771 feet and takes its name from the Irish for "deer", forms part of the Slieve Gullion ring dyke complex. Its underlying rock is a quartz porphyry which on its south-eastern slope appear as dykes in the earlier silurian rock. Dykes of diorite and felsite also exist, described as "peculiar in its composition and exceedingly rare in its occurrence". Another feature of Feede are the striations caused by the ice-cap which indicate that in this area the ice moved almost due north to south compared with the north-west to south-east movement in the Carlingford Lough areas. These striations give the roche moutonnée appearance to Feede, with the rock outcrop shaped and rendered smooth by the passing ice.

At the bottom of the south-eastern slope a complex of pre-historic cairns exists at Aghnaskeagh, containing archeological evidence of the successive Neolithic, Bronze and Iron Ages. It consists of a court cairn, a portal tomb and six Bronze Age cists. The Iron Age smelting was conducted in a furnace area immediately north of the portal tomb.

Ravensdale

Feede Hill

With thanks to Exitex

Dundalk - Town and People

By 800 A.D., the southern part of the kingdom of the Connaille comprising Cúailgne and Magh Muirthemne had become detached from Magh Cobha and had emerged as the small autonomous kingdom of the Connaille Muirthemne. The list of the kings of the Connaille indicates that it survived as a kingdom until the early twelfth century when it was annexed by the larger kingdom of the Airghialla to the west. Settlement about Dundalk at this period consisted of a string of small communities located on the high ground, enclosing the inner reaches of Dundalk Bay. Archeological evidence suggests that this area has been in continuous occupation from the Bronze Age, with the ringforts and souterrains of the early Christian period of the Connaille Muirthemne to be found in all locations. The area eastward from Castletown Mount on which the modern town now stands was the site of Aonach Muirthemne. An Aonach was a place where the people of a locality used to assemble from time to time to enact laws or to discharge other business of public importance for the community. It was also a place for sports and entertainment or used as a fair for the buying and selling of produce. That this place was an Aonach is testified by several stories from the Ulster Cycle in each of which the place is referred to as an Aonach. The poet Yeats adapted three of these stories, "The Only Jealousy of Emer", "The Death of Connla" and "Baile's Strand", all of which date from between A.D. 800 and A.D.1100 as verse plays. The last of these takes its name from the original name of the strand, Traige Baile Mac Buan i.e., the Strand of Baile son of Buan, Baile being referred to in the story as the son of the king of Uladh or Ulster. This strand consisted of a beach formed between two gravel ridges, one of which extends eastwards on the south bank of the Castletown river to Soldiers' Point; the other from west of the Big Bridge southwards via Clanbrassil St. and Park St. to Dublin St. and the Dublin Road. The strand seems to have been connected to the high ground at Ballybarrack and Castletown by roadways known in later documents respectively as Cassangarrow [the rough path] and Balagh Carbit [chariot or cart way], each leading to the harbour of Athlon or Broad Ford located in Seatown.

Town & People

The coming of the Normans to Ulster in the late twelfth century totally shattered the polity of east Ulster including Louth. The first incursion took place in 1177 when John de Courcy, moving northwards through Meath and Louth, attacked and captured Downpatrick. After further battles involving most of the northern Irish the latter were defeated leaving de Courcy master of the greater parts of the counties of Down and Antrim. De Courcy's interests did not extend to North Louth, then comprised within the kingdom of the Airghialla under Murchadh O'Carroll. After Murchadh's death in 1188-89 the Norman occupation of Louth was proceeded with, probably on the basis of a plan conceived when Henry II's son John visited Ireland in 1185. He had in his retinue two men, Bertram de Verdon and Gilbert de Pippard, who remained in Ireland after John's return to England. When Louth was taken over by the crown lordship in 1189 it was divided between these men, only excepting the lands about Louth village, later the barony of Louth. De Verdon's share consisted of north and south Louth later known as the baronies of Dundalk, Cooley and Ferrard.

The first Norman settlement in Dundalk was at Castletown where de Verdon had the motte castle at the Mount constructed c1185-90. Here he granted a charter to St. John the Baptist's Church of Dundalk of all the tithes and other benefices of his lands about Dundalk and which included such places as the lands of the Burgages, Ballriggan, Athlon and Ballybarrack but excluding 'Aschacmnacharan [Haggardstown] and five carucates pertaining to Kilkerley'. The reference to the lands of the Burgages indicates that a borough corporation had also been established at this period. This was the Corporation of Dundalk to which Bertram, according to a later document, made "divers burgesses and enfeoffed them of divers burgages with tenements of the said town with commons of pasture, to hold undivided forever without paying any rent or service whatever". The location of the first township was at Castletown, probably on the northeastern slope of the Mount between the motte and Castletown graveyard. While these developments were taking place at Castletown, a township had also begun to evolve at Tráige Baile Mac Búan later to become known in legal documents as the Villa Marina or Seatown. About 1185 the monastery and hospital of St. Leonard's were founded here, reputedly by Bertram de Verdon under the auspices of the Hospitaller Order of the Crossbearers. In 1246, a Franciscan Friary had also been established at Seatown, reputedly by John de Verdon, the remains of which still survive as "Seatown Castle".

In the early thirteenth century another development took place in the form of an unwalled Sráid Bhaile or "Street-town" which was built along the strand and the high ground of the gravel ridge leading southwards from the Big Bridge. This "Sráid Bhaile Dún Dealgan" as it became known to the Irish, may have followed the line of an earlier path or roadway on the ridge connecting Cassangarrow with Balagh Carbit and a ford across the river adjacent to the site of the present Big Bridge. Another roadway, leading from the harbour area via the present day Chapel St. to Yorke St. thence to Cam or Crooked St. (now Nicholas St. and Wolfe Tone Terrace), connected with Balagh Carbit via John's St. This complex of roadways was to become the street plan of the new town, the principal characteristic of which was its conformity to the topography created by the underlying gravel ridges. By the middle of the thirteenth century, this new town had come into being, incorporating the area north of the Market Square to include Clanbrassil St., Church St., Bridge St. and the areas to the east incorporating Nicholas St. and Yorke St. That this was a planned development is indicated by the division of the area into burgage plots many of which can still be identified. That it was a continuum with the earlier settlement in Castletown is indicated by the name given to it in

the early fourteenth century common seal of the town, the "Nove Ville De Dundalk", or the "New Town of Dundalk". The parish church, which would have been founded at this time, still stands, albeit in a much altered state, as the church of St. Nicholas, now the parish church of the Church of Ireland of Dundalk.

By the beginning of the fourteenth century the New Town of Dundalk had been firmly established, and was enclosed by a town wall which ran along by the river bank on the north side to the present day St. Nicholas Terrace, and thence southwards along De La Salle Terrace and the Long Walk to the rear of the Post Office, thence eastwards across the Market Square to the rear of the houses fronting the street. The eastern section of the New Town bounding with Seatown was left unwalled but in the fifteenth century a deep trench, intended to carry seawater around the town, was constructed which also enclosed the earlier walling to the west. This development is an indication of the importance of Dundalk at this period both as a market town and as a bastion for the defence of the Norman, later English settlements in North Louth against the marauding Irishry of Ulster. There were four gates in the walled area, two on the north, the Blind gate at the entrance to Linenhall St. and the North gate at the entrance to the Big Bridge. A third called the Castletown gate stood at the western end of John's St. while the fourth or Warren's gate stood across the Market Square at the junction with Clanbrassil St.. There were two gates on the town trench the first called Staff-lane gate at the junction of York St. and Chapel St. and the second or Upper Seatown gate, which stood in the Roden Place area of the town.

The English colonisation of Louth had been completed by the early part of the thirteenth century. Known as Uriel [Airghialla] or English Uriel to distinguish it from Irish Airghialla to the west in County Monaghan, the land had been parceled out to the new arrivals, the incoming tenants of the de Verdons, while still more settled as burgesses in the new town of Dundalk. Many of the new settlers came from Staffordshire, where the de Verdons had their English estates, and from the contiguous areas of Derbyshire and Cheshire. Most of the ancient Connaille, from whom the local surname Connolly seems to be derived, fled west into Airghialla; those that remained became "betaghs" on the de Verdon lands about Dundalk. A betagh or, "biatach" in Irish, was an unfree or "base client" whose role under old Irish law was that of 'provider of food' i.e., an unfree rent paying tenant akin to the English villein. There is

some evidence that betagh settlements were made in the Kilkerley-Ballybarrack and Haggardstown areas of North Louth and this may explain the exclusion of these areas from de Verdon's charter to the parish of St. John the Baptist of Castletown.

In 1312, Uriel was seriously disturbed by an uprising of the colonists against the crown lordship in Dublin. Described at the time as the insurrection of the men of Dundalk and Machaire Connaille, this obscure event, which was led by the elite of town and county, seems to have originated from purely local grievances, the details of which are now lost. By this date the chief lords of the settlement in County Louth were absentees, leaving the colonists to fend for themselves in a hostile society where a resurgent Irishry had become as aggressive as their colonial neighbours. The latter, turned in on themselves and defensive in outlook, sought political ascendancy not compromise as the best means of ensuring their survival. While at the same time protesting their loyalty, they were fractious in their dealings with the crown lordship, even to the point of rebellion. A peace was eventually patched up and while fines were levied, the colonists appear to have avoided outright defeat. In May 1315, Edward Bruce, brother of Robert, King of Scotland, landed at

Larne, County Antrim with an army of 6,000 men and by the 29th June they were encamped on the southern slope of the hill of Faughart. His objective was to wrest the kingship of Ireland from the English. Opposing him were the "lordis of that cuntre" assembled at Dundalk under their leaders, including erstwhile rebels such as Milo, Nicholas and Robert de Verdon. After preliminary skirmishing, Bruce's advance party reported that the enemy would, "only be a half dinner to them". The Scots were drawn up in two battalions "with banneris all displayit" when the defenders launched an attack. After a heavy engagement, the latter broke against an onslaught by Bruce of such force that, in their retreat into the town by the Castletown gate, the Scots in hot pursuit accompanied them. The vanguard of the latter led by Sir Thomas Randolf made such a slaughter and "so cruel a slaying" that the streets "all bludy war [were] of slain men that war liand [lying] thar". The town was extensively burned and pillaged, the Franciscan Friary ransacked and its community of thirty-one friars killed. For the next three years Louth suffered from further attacks by Bruce, and in October 1318 he was again encamped at Faughart where he was confronted by a large force under Sir John de Bermingham including Sir Milo and Sir Walter de Verdon, John de Cusack of Dromin and Sir Walter de la Pulle, whose contingent included John Maupas the man reputed to have killed Bruce. On the 14th October, battle was joined at the hill of Faughart. At first the battle favoured Bruce, who overran the English encampment at the Annies where they gained "a rich booty together with provisions and equipment for war". This was followed by a lull in the fighting during which John Maupas, disguised as "a shameless idiot", infiltrated Bruce's camp and coming on Bruce, killed him by trickery, "scattering his brains" around the hill. In the ensuing confusion the English launched their attack "making terrible slaughter" on the Scots. So ended Bruce's career in Ireland, described in the Annals of the Four Masters as "the destroyer of the people of Ireland in general both English and Irish". In the wake of the defeat at Faughart the victor John de Bermingham was created an earl and granted Louth as a liberty. Being an outsider, his rule was resented by the local community. Once again they asserted their independence by attacking de Bermingham at his residence at Braganstown in 1329 where they murdered him along with one hundred and sixty of his followers. The perpetrators of this atrocity, which included some who had participated in the earlier rebellion, were never punished. Thereafter, the colonists were left alone, the authorities in Dublin evidently satisfied to have such a warlike community established on the northern march with the Irish of Ulster.

Chronic warfare did not impede the growth of Dundalk and if at times the colonists were at odds with the authorities in Dublin, civil government was nevertheless practiced in the town where courts, civil and ecclesiastical, administered the law at regular intervals. In 1311, it was alleged in court that William Brisbon of Castlering and his two brothers were given sanctuary in the Franciscan Friary after an affray at Allardstown where the sheriff, Richard Gernon, was killed. It was reported that the miscreants enjoyed the hospitality of the friars for fourteen days, "the whole town knowing of it", before making good their escape. In 1379, the archbishop Sweteman issued a decree in a matrimonial cause concerning an Agnes Laundey of Dundalk who was alleged to have married three men, "who were still living" and had been guilty of adultery with a John While for about twelve years. Having been found guilty, she was sentenced "as a corporal penance" to be "beaten around the churches for twelve years".

John Drumming, William Hobbeson and William Birle described as "foreign merchants", took an important case touching the rights of Dundalk Corporation to regulate the markets of the town in 1378. They pleaded that from a time beyond the memory of man [i.e. before 1189] each and every merchant, not only of Dundalk, "but strangers also" had the right to sell "English cloth" in the town without hindrance. In response the Corporation claimed that no foreign merchant, nor anyone other than a burgess of the town and living in the town, since time beyond the memory of man, could bring salt or linen cloth, untanned hides or other merchandise for retailing without license of the bailiffs. The case was tried before a jury and perhaps not surprisingly the Corporation won the day.

Throughout the fifteenth century, the lordship of Ireland was effectively reduced to the areas immediately surrounding Dublin city and county, known as the English Pale, with Louth divided into two distinct parts. To the south and east of a line from Dundalk through Darver and Ardee to Drumconrath the lands were in the English Pale, while to the north and west lay the March, where the Englishry and the Irishry lived cheek by jowl in a chronic state of dispute for power and ascendancy. Between 1420 and 1450 Eoghan O'Neill of Tyrone and the English of North Louth, under Sir John Bellew of Roche, were in constant conflict over land ownership. In 1444 the Irish sacked the unwalled Sraidbhaile of

Dundalk [Seatown], agreeing to spare the rest of the town on payment of sixty marks and two 'tuns' of wine. In 1452, Eoghan O'Neill invaded North Louth and two years later Richard Bellew was ordered by proclamation to appear before the Council in Dublin on pain of forfeiture of his estate. Reluctant to appear he explained that his lands were situated on the frontiers of the march contiguous to O'Neill and, because of the war then subsisting between "the king's faithful subjects and O'Neill", he could not respond to the proclamation. He managed to patch up his affairs with the Council by 1458 and in 1463 he obtained a subsidy of £10 to repair his castle at Roche and in 1472 had another subsidy of £10 to "erect a tower or pile at Castletown". The latter stands to this day on the grounds of the St. Louis convent schools at Castletown.

With the advent of the Tudor era after 1485, a greater concentration on Irish affairs developed with the Irish Lordship seeking the establishment of strong central government control and the reduction of the powers of local magnates and factions. In 1524, the leading gentry of the March were summoned to Dublin to enter into recognisances to keep the peace and to make restitution "for all manners of thefts, robberies, trespass, extortions, riots, oppressions and for all other offenses that may be restored or compensated by pecunial sums". Included in the list from North Louth were James Gernon of Killencoole, Walter Bellew of Roche, Patrick Gernon of Gernonstown, Thomas Babe of Darver, Christopher Taaffe of Stevenstown, George Gernon of Milltown, Robert Gernon of Mayne, Oliver Plunkett of Tallanstown, William Bellew of Verdonstown and Phillip Bellew of Haynestown. When Anthony St.Leger succeeded as lord deputy in 1541, a policy of reform and rapprochement was introduced, bringing about a short-lived peace to the March, after Con Bacach O'Neill of Tyrone had made his submission and accepted the earldom of Tyrone from the king. He named his son Matthew as his heir with the courtesy title of Baron Dungannon. Matthew had been born in Dundalk of Alison Kelly, the wife of the local blacksmith and, until his sixteenth year he was accepted as Kelly's son. After Kelly died Alison brought Matthew to Dungannon where she presented him to Con Bacach as his son. As Shane O'Neill, Con Bacach's legitimate son, was to describe it, Matthew's mother "for vain glory and for a name to herself declared him to be O'Neill's son, alleging and boasting of her unhappiness, how that O'Neill lay once with her. And O'Neill being a man that never refused no child that any woman named to be his, and he had divers besides the said Matthew, accepted and took him to be his son". This fateful decision was to wreak havoc in the marchlands of southeast Ulster including North Louth as Shane O'Neill, coming to his majority, led a revolt against his father. Subsequently this spread into North Louth and Dundalk, where Con Bacach and Matthew found refuge from time to time and where some or all of Matthew's sons, Brian, Art, Cormac and Hugh may have been born. Following Shane O'Neill's death in 1567, Matthew's son Hugh succeeded as Baron Dungannon and, in 1575, to the earldom of Tyrone.

Hugh O'Neill's relationships with the lord deputy Fitzwilliam began to deteriorate after 1590. Throughout the next five or six years conferences were held in and about Dundalk during which, representatives of the Irish Council met representatives of the northern Irish led by O'Neill, in successive vain attempts at rapprochement. O'Neill also laid claim to the ownership of a castle in Dundalk, giving rise to a dispute, the report of which provides us with a glimpse of the town as it existed at this period. A castle known as Rothes castle stood on a commanding site at the junction of Clanbrassil St. and Church St. where the Dublin House licensed premises now stands. On the 30th April 1594,

O'Neill took possession of the castle and when Sir Henry Duke the town governor became aware of what had happened he sent for the town bailiffs who took possession of the castle in the name of the Corporation. O'Neill reacted by way of a written complaint to the Council in Dublin, claiming that he had "lately the possession of a castle at Dundalk whereunto none hath better right to" than himself and which had been taken from him by the bailiffs. Deputy Fitzwilliam in a report to Lord Burghley dated May 1594, stressed the strategic importance of Dundalk and of Rothes castle which, he claimed, commanded the principal street of the town "from end to end" to the north gate, "so as a chicken cannot stir that way but is in danger". Informed of O'Neill's complaint, Duke responded with a report dated the 9th June which was accompanied by "a Plott" or map of the situation of the castle and the "chiefest" part of the town. The "Plott" is a perspective drawing of the town from its eastern aspect showing Warren's gate on the south with present day Clanbrassil St. curving north to join with Church St.. At the latter junction stood the market cross in the middle of the street, directly opposite Rothe's castle which as Duke explained had a commanding position in the town centre. Directly east from the castle and the market cross were Stafflane, now Yorke St. and its gate "being the way from the cross to the windmills at the seashore". Standing at the entrance to Stafflane stood Rothes Castle on the south and the Tholsel or House of Assembly [i.e., guildhall] on the north. At the north end of Church St. stood a bar or "cross-wall adjoining Mr. Brandon's house". Mr. Cashell's house is also shown, evidently a substantial mansion, which stood on the site of the present-day Dundalk House, and was the place where government representatives stayed when visiting the town. Unfortunately, O'Neill's claim, which seems to have been based upon a right of inheritance from his grandmother Alison, was not pursued. In a letter dated 8th February 1560/6l Shane O'Neill had complained that "the said Matthew should inherit my father's lands and also to inherit his own rightful father the smith's and his mother's lands within the town of Dundalk which the said Matthew's son hath possession". Clearly the O'Neills were intimately associated with Dundalk in the sixteenth century. Hugh's brother Art claimed on one occasion that "their ancestors and especially themselves had been bred and brought up there".

On the 23rd June, O'Neill was proclaimed traitor at the market cross of Dundalk. Over the next three years a desultory warfare was carried out, punctuated by periods of truce. However, after O'Neill's victory at the battle of the Yellow Ford in August 1598, and the failed expedition of the earl of Essex in 1599, it became evident to the English that outright war was the only way to subdue O'Neill. The task was given to Charles Blount Lord Mountjoy who landed in Dublin as lord deputy in February 1600. In October 1600, Mountjoy was at Dundalk where he conducted a muster of his forces in the main street of the town [Clanbrassil St]. In October the entire force moved northwards to Faughart where they advanced through the Moiry Pass and, after a hot skirmish with O'Neill, reached the garrison town of Newry. For the next three years Dundalk was heavily garrisoned while much of the campaigning was done elsewhere. In Ulster a policy of total warfare led to widespread famine especially in the vicinity of garrisons such as Newry and Carrickfergus. O'Neill's surrender at Mellifont in March 1603 brought the war to an end and ushered in a new era for Dundalk as for Ulster.

In the last few decades of the sixteenth century a perceptible change took place in the relationships between the old colonists and the new arrivals from England who came in as soldiers and officials under a succession of English born deputies and lieutenants. The newcomers, dubbed the "New English" by their remote cousins the

"Old English", gradually dislodged the latter as the ruling elite, a process of alienation which was further exacerbated by the more fundamental distinction of religion. The New English were predominantly Protestant while the Old English were almost exclusively Catholic. Despite a Protestant presence in the town, Dundalk remained Catholic throughout this period and while an attempt was made to enforce attendance at Protestant services in the early years of James I, this was unsuccessful and the law fell into disuse. In 1618 a Catholic place of worship in the town was large enough to hold a congregation of seven hundred people where two Franciscans gave a mission throughout the Lenten period. In 1635, William Brereton described Dundalk as a town of strength and a walled town. He found that one of the bailiffs was a "Papist" and that the greater part of the population was "Popishly affected".

At this time Dundalk was a reasonably prosperous market town and by the late sixteenth century had extended further southwards into a walled area known as the "Upper-end" better known today as Park St.. The Rampart River was also a development of this period. The insurrection of 1641 marked a major turning point in the history of the town. Within days of the outbreak, Dundalk fell without a blow struck by the townspeople. In April 1642 the crown forces broke the siege of Drogheda and, under their commander Sir Henry Tichborne, marched northwards and after a sharp encounter captured Dundalk. Retribution swiftly followed, several of the members of the Corporation were summarily hanged and the town subjected to four days of systematic pillage.

In a real sense Tichborne's sack of the town brought an end to the Old English community of Dundalk. Throughout the ensuing years of warfare the town was heavily garrisoned by a succession of forces, at first by troops loyal to the crown and later by a Parliamentarian regiment, shipped in from Liverpool. In May 1649, the town was re-taken by troops loyal to the crown the major part of the garrison going over to the latter. Amongst these was a Colonel Mark Trevor of Rostrevor County Down. He had served in England as a royalist and was colonel of a horse regiment at the battle of Marsdon Moor. He later returned to Ireland and, following Ormond's surrender in 1647, transferred his allegiance to the parliamentarians. He was however a closet-royalist and it was not surprising that he deserted to Ormond at the first opportunity. After Cromwell's storming of Drogheda in August 1649 the town was occupied, without resistance, by a force detached from Drogheda under Colonel Venables. All the houses and lands of the Corporation were then confiscated and rented out, mainly to soldiers, until 1659 when Cromwell's son Henry leased the entire estate to Colonel Mark Trevor, who later had it re-granted to him under the Restoration land settlement. A rent-roll and contemporary maps of this period give a detailed picture of the town showing the three divisions as already described. The Corporation estate included eight castles and two hundred and forty houses including cabins. The Upper End where most of the cabins were located, was ruinous as were the John's St. and Cam St. areas. While a number of the names in the rent-roll were Irish, mainly living in the cabins, very few were Old English. Ex-soldiers and other New English settlers occupied the choice properties however. The Old English made some recoveries during the Restoration period, but later rent-rolls reveal that the population mix established during the period of the English Commonwealth persisted into the eighteenth century. The town had barely recovered from the warfare of the 1640's and 1650's when the Williamite revolt of 1688 was begun. In August 1689, a Williamite army under General Schomberg occupied the town and was opposed by an army under James II deployed along the Fane River. The latter did not

attack, but Schomberg's advance was stopped and, for want of supplies, became bogged down. His army was then beset by an epidemic of fever and had to evacuate to Belfast leaving the dead and dying lying around in the streets. In June, James II returned to Dundalk but, upon the arrival of the forces of William of Orange in the Moiry Pass, James gave orders to retire southwards. Before doing so his men plundered the town. The Williamites found it "wholly desolate" and, on the 29th June as they marched out to "Boyne Waters" they met "no living creatures" along the way other than "some starving creatures near a mill scraping for food in a dust heap of chaff and husks".

The town made a slow recovery from the effects of the Williamite wars. The Trevors sold their interests in the town to a James Hamilton of Tollymore, County Down who died in 1701, leaving his widow Anne and a teen-age son James. James Hamilton was educated at Oxford and later was M.P. for Dundalk in the years 1715 to 1719 at which point he was created Viscount Limerick. He was also an M.P. in the English Parliament from 1735 to 1754 and was created earl of Clanbrassil in 1756. He married a Dutch woman, Henrietta Bentinck at The Hague in 1729. In addition to this, in 1721 he agreed to establish a grammar school and to construct a harbour for the town. He fulfiled these obligations and by 1736 was further involved in the establishment of a public corporation for the manufacture of cambric linen in Dundalk. With assistance from the Linen Board, the manufactory was erected at Parliament Square now Aiken Military Barracks.

The establishment of the cambric manufactory began a period of over twenty years, during which a complete transformation took place in Dundalk. Evidently working to a comprehensive re-development plan, Vicount Limerick had the town walls, gates and castles demolished. The stone and rubble were then used to erect a sea-rampart, enclosing the area of the South March from the sea and, by other drainage improvements, hundreds of acres on the south and east of the town were reclaimed. The main streets were gradually re-developed by means of covenants in the building leases requiring premises to be built according to certain specifications. In 1740, a new sessions house was erected on the site of the present Courthouse to form the eastern end of a new Market Square. On the western end a corn-market house was constructed. The other two sides were filled by commercial buildings, including an inn, which still stands. A new road network was laid out, all leading eastwards from the main streets. These

included the Quay Rd. now St. Mary's Road leading to the harbour pier at St. Helena and a road from the Market Square to the cambric manufactory at Parliament Square. The third was a long avenue off the Dublin Road eastwards to the Red Barns now the Avenue Road. The western area was reserved for a large demesne extending westwards to Castletown including a formal, ornamental garden in the immediate environs of Dundalk House, Lord Limerick's residence at Church St.. This was described in 1752 as having some fine plantations and walks, an artificial serpentine river, a china bridge and a fine kitchen garden with closets of fruits. In 1750 Lord Limerick gave a site for the erection of a Roman Catholic Chapel at Chapel St. which survived as the parish church until St. Patrick's was opened in 1842.

A branch of the United Irish Society was established in the town in the 1790's as well as a branch of the Catholic secret society known as the Defenders. Following the proscription of the former, the membership of both merged into the secret society of the United Irishmen in 1794. These developments were but a reflection of what was taking place in Ulster where, in March 1797, General Lake issued a proclamation calling for the surrender of arms. It was the enforcement of this proclamation which precipitated the subsequent insurrection. The town of Dundalk did not escape; the military engaging in arbitrary arrests, courts martial and indiscriminate public floggings at the Market Square.

In 1801 the two kingdoms of Britain and Ireland were united under one legislature as the United Kingdom of Great Britain and Ireland. In 1799 Lord Cornwallis visited Dundalk where he received, as he had expected, an address from the Corporation in favour of the Union, but was surprised when he received a similar address from the local Catholic parish priest supported by several of his more influential parishioners. This apparent unanimity sprang from entirely differing motivations. The former saw the proposed union as a means for the continuance of Protestant ascendancy in Ireland, while the latter saw the union as a means of securing Catholic Emancipation. However, a dissident point of view was expressed at a public meeting in January 1800, at which a resolution was adopted condemning the proposed union as fraught with the most pernicious consequences.

The opening decade of the nineteenth century was a period of economic boom for Dundalk as demand for agricultural produce soared on the world market. All this was to change with the ending of the Napoleonic Wars in 1815. By 1817, the value of exports through Dundalk had fallen from £345,638 in 1812, to £70,000 with consequential effects on agriculture, trade and industry. To add to the general miseries, a famine, followed by an epidemic of typhus broke out, resulting in widespread suffering and destitution.

As the town recovered, new industries began to appear. Kelly's Brewery was taken over and converted into a distillery and on the north side of the Market Square an Alexander Sheckleton, who invented the first portable steam engine, established an engineering works, which was later expanded by a succession of owners. Two tobacco making firms were established, one in Earl St. which survived until 1853 and the other at Church St. which grew and prospered as P.J.Carrolls and Co. until recently taken over by a multinational corporation.

The varying eras of prosperity enjoyed by Dundalk throughout the nineteenth century is perhaps best expressed in the quality of the public and commercial buildings erected in this period. These range from the neo-classical Courthouse (with its portico modelled on the temple of Thesius in Athens) to St. Patrick's Church

Town & People

modelled on King's College Cambridge and Bath Abbey in England to the Victorian extravaganza of Duffy's Hardware, at No.70 Clanbrassil St.. No.70 is a good example of the commercial buildings erected in Dundalk during the 1830's to the 1860's. It was built as a wine store in 1868 to a design by John Neville, the County Surveyor, and stands out as the most ornate of the buildings constituting the Clanbrassil St. façades. The building of the Courthouse was commenced in 1813, but was not completed until 1819. St. Patrick's Church was a product of the post-Emancipation period when at last the Catholic parish could express itself without inhibition. Commenced in 1837, it was opened for worship in 1842 and completed in the famine year of 1847.

The quality of the public and commercial buildings of this period concealed a darker existence in the town of widespread poverty, wretched and insanitary housing conditions and endemic fevers such as smallpox and typhus. The houses of the poor, who were a substantial part of the population, consisted of one to two-roomed cabins of flimsy construction, grossly overcrowded and grouped in terraces in off-street lanes and yards or at the entrances to the town. In 1837 it was reported that the poor of the town

were "suffering much privation", their food consisting chiefly of salt fish, milk, potatoes and oatmeal. Fuel was scarce and the clothing worn was a coarse frieze, "poverty and distress abound and our Society is frequently compelled to witness scenes of wretchedness calculated to awaken painful feelings". The report concluded, "much of this depends on the want of employment, of education, moral culture and on the early and ruinous habits of intoxication".

In 1832, a Town Commission was established in Dundalk with powers to appoint a town watch or civil police force, the provision of public lighting and footpath repair, the scavenging of houses and the removal of domestic waste. In 1854, under new legislation, more extensive powers were granted to town commissions which enabled the Dundalk Commissioners to embark on more extensive measures of town improvements. These included the provision of a piped water supply, the laying of a public sewerage system and land reclamations along the Castletown river bank resulting in what are now the Fairgreen and St. Helena's Park areas. Other innovations included: the provision of a municipal theatre, a public library service, the removal of fairs from the public streets, the closure of the old burial grounds at the Green Church and St. Leonard's in

Seatown and, in conjunction with the Board of Guardians, the establishment of the Joint Burial Board and burial ground at Dowdallshill.

The Urban District Council replaced the Commissioner system in 1899 and commenced the first public housing projects in the town at Castletown Rd. and Seatown. In 1911 they established a municipal electricity undertaking which continued in use until taken over by the E.S.B. in the 1930's.

In 1846, it was reported of the town that "all the short lanes and narrow alleys as well as parts of the main streets are of a poor filthy and wretched character. The town contains some good shops and very many tolerable houses but is burdened and filtified as much as not a few second-rate Irish towns with dismal lanes and squalid suburbs." This was Dundalk on the eve of the great famine.

While Dundalk did not suffer famine conditions to the same extent as other parts of the county, the years between 1845 and 1850 were grim years for the towns underclass, the labouring poor. In February 1846, in anticipation of increased admissions, the Workhouse established in 1842, ordered additional bedding and in March there were 36 admissions on one day alone, "nearly all in a state of starvation". In the following month potatoes were taken off the diet and did not return again until late 1849, bread being substituted. By this time the Workhouse had over 500 inmates in a building intended for 200. The inevitable outbreak of disease followed. In March 1846 an epidemic outbreak of fever occurred, necessitating the provision of fever hospital accommodation. In October 1847, fever was again rampant. In March 1847, road relief schemes were initiated in Dundalk and Cooley. In October a scheme of outdoor relief was instituted at the rate of seven pence per week for an adult and three and a half-pence per child. A soup kitchen scheme also operated in Dundalk where, in 1847, over thirteen per cent of the population was served until it was closed down in January 1848. In May 1849, probably in connection with the cholera epidemic when 20 deaths per week were recorded, local health committees were established in Dundalk, Louth, Barronstown, Ravensdale and Carlingford.

Throughout the earlier part of the century, trade through the port had been impeded by the inadequacy of the harbour facilities and, in 1837 an Act was passed providing for the establishment of a Harbour Commission. In 1840, a major

Town & People

scheme of harbour improvements was commenced and completed in 1848. The centrepiece of the scheme was the construction of a new channel from Soldiers' Point to the inner harbour, a distance of over one mile. In 1845, the Dundalk to Enniskillen Railway Company was established in Seatown, with a railway works in Barrack St.. The section of the line from Barrack St. to Castleblaney was completed in February 1849, finally reaching Enniskillen in 1859. Other contemporary railway developments were the Dublin to Drogheda line in 1844 and the Dublin Belfast Junction Railway which reached Dundalk in 1849 and continued northwards to join the Ulster Railway at Portadown. By 1875 all of these railway companies had amalgamated into the Great Northern Railway Company with a railway complex extending throughout Ulster. In 1880, Dundalk was selected as the centre for the engineering works to service the new complex, a development which was to be the backbone of the prosperity of the town until the 1950's.

Throughout the nineteenth century, town politics were at all times vigorous and robust. In 1842 and 1843 mass meetings, held by Daniel O'Connell in support of repeal of the Union were attended by over 60,000 people. That separation from Britain was not the motivation of these meetings is evidenced by the fact that an archway across Clanbrassil St. had pictures of Queen Victoria and Prince Albert, while a banner at a banquet proclaimed "Long live Victoria Queen of our affections". From the 1870's demand for Home Rule was the dominant political issue but the split in the Nationalist party following the O'Shea divorce proceedings, deeply divided the politics of the town. Although not perceived at the time, the period that followed was to be a watershed in Irish politics in that the movement for political separation from Britain was sparked off afresh. In 1907, a local branch of Sinn Fein was founded in Dundalk. At this early period Sinn Fein was a non-violent non-political organisation transformed subsequently by the forces set loose by the Home Rule controversies. Mr. Patrick Hughes of Park St. was chairman in 1910. He later led the breakaway Irish Volunteers in Dundalk and, in Easter week 1916, commanded a detachment of over one hundred men to Dublin to participate in the insurrection. They failed to reach the city and on their return to Dundalk were rounded up and imprisoned. In the elections of 1918, the local Sinn Fein candidate J.J. Kelly had a landslide victory and attended the first meeting of Dail Eireann in January 1919, the resolutions of which conferred a political legitimacy for the war of independence which followed. During the latter, North Louth was the scene of several ambushes resulting in the death or injury of policemen, military and their auxiliaries. There were also reprisals, including the burning down of houses and other property owned by known I.R.A. men. With the signing of the Treaty in December 1921, the war came to an end. The political controversies which followed the treaty brought division into the ranks of those who had participated in the war of independence including the membership of the Fourth Northern Division of the I.R.A. in whose area North Louth was located. Their leader, Frank Aiken, attempted to follow a neutral course but with the commencement of the Civil War on the 29th June this was no longer possible. Having demurred from arresting sections of his Division who sided with the anti-treaty forces, Aiken was himself arrested and the military barracks occupied by pro-treaty forces of the provisional government. On the 27th July anti-treaty elements attacked the jail, releasing Aiken and other prisoners and on the 14th August they attacked and occupied the military barracks. The Provisional Government reacted by dispatching a force northward to re-take the town. On the 16th August, the latter arrived on the southern and western approaches where they prepared to attack. This was avoided when Aiken withdrew

northwards enabling the Provisional Government forces to occupy the town. Soon afterwards the rest of North Louth was re-taken albeit that guerrilla warfare continued until the Civil War ended in April 1923.

The decade which followed the ending of the Civil War was for Dundalk a period of economic recession while the hostilities engendered by the Civil War divided society and political unrest was never far from the surface. However, as the decade progressed and the government became more confident, conditions began to improve. The establishment of the Fianna Fail party in 1926 was a major turning point bringing those who had opposed the treaty in the Civil War back to a constitutional path. In 1933, having attained an overall majority in the Dail, they took over the reins of power. The transition was accomplished without a hitch and, in the rising tide of the relative prosperity which followed, they were able to accomplish much both for the economy as well as improvements in social conditions. A policy of industrial protectionism, using external tariffs, enabled several new industries to be established in the town, notably the boot and shoe industry. Through the medium of the Urban District Council, major housing projects were initiated progressively eliminating slum conditions and providing housing for an ever-increasing population.

Following the outbreak of the war in 1939, the government decided to follow a path of neutrality and in view of the uncertainty of the times declared an 'Emergency'. Scarcities of food and fuel and the ever-present threat of invasion, by one side or the other of the combatants, induced a form of introversion into society, which was accompanied also by a widespread sense of togetherness and unity. The huge numbers of persons of all classes and creeds who flocked to the ranks of the emergency army and to the other voluntary aid bodies such as the L.D.F. the A.R.P. and the Red Cross expressed this. This spirit of growing unity was particularly noticeable in Dundalk where past dissension, whether political or religious, was laid aside and, in the words of a popular song of the time, a "step together" spirit imbued the whole community.

In the half century which has elapsed since the ending of the Second World War, the population of Dundalk has increased by 40% from 18,562 in 1946 to 25,842 in 1991. This increase has taken place against a background of change in the industrial and commercial sectors, brought on by changes in technology and in world market conditions. Ranked among the casualties was the Dundalk Railway Works, closed in 1958. A succession of engineering companies continued to use the works throughout the following decade finally ending with the failure and liquidation of the S.& S. Company in 1968. Another casualty was the boot and shoe industry. This was from the outset a tariff-protected industry but with the onset of free trade and our entry into the European Economic Community, the industry gradually declined and, while two factories still survive, the larger firms have been liquidated. On the other hand, the brewing industry has survived and prospered, not only the long-established company of Macardle Moore but also the Harp Lager Brewery, founded in the late 1950's in what was the former Northern brewery. In the past fifteen to twenty years a new industrial complex has begun to emerge, helping to fill the gap created by the closure of the older industries. Dundalk town and district has many attractions not only for industry but also for tourism. It is at the centre of an area of fifty miles radius in which 2,000,000 people live and is serviced by modern road, rail and shipping facilities. It is also within a one-hour drive from the two international airports of Belfast and Dublin. The establishment of the Regional Technical College has provided a steady stream of graduates to work on the shop floors and in the offices of the new industrial centres, which is also serviced by the local offices of the industrial development and labour market organisations of the public service.

It was inevitable that with its close proximity to the border with Northern Ireland, Dundalk would be perceived by many as lying in a politically disturbed area. This is not so. As is the case for many parts of Northern Ireland itself, Dundalk and North Louth have not been involved in the turmoils that have beset the north over the past twenty-five years. The neglect of border areas, which is a feature not unknown in other member states of the European Union is gradually being addressed through Interregge and other E.U. programmes and by the International Fund for Ireland. There is also a great deal of cross border co-operation developing, especially in the immediate border areas, where recognition of the existence of common problems is growing and where people are coming together to find solutions.

While unemployment is still high in Dundalk, there is a growing confidence that the industrial doldrums of the 1975-1985 period will not be re-visited and that the town will regain its industrial prosperity.

Bibliography

Buckley Victor M. & Sweetman P. David, Archaeological Survey of County Louth, Stationery Office, Dublin 1991

Byrne Francis John, Irish Kings and High Kings, Batsford 1973

Casey Christine & Rowan Alister, The Buildings of Ireland North Leinster, Penguin Books 1993

Gavin Joseph & O'Sullivan Harold , Dundalk: A Military History, Dundalgan Press 1987

Gillespie Raymond & O'Sullivan Harold, The Borderlands Essays on the History of the Ulster-Leinster Borders, Institute of Irish Studies, Belfast 1989

Gogarty Thomas, St. Mary's Abbey Louth, Louth Arch. & Hist. Journal IV No.2

Gosling Paul, From Dun Delca to Dundalk A.D. c1187-1700, Louth Arch. & Hist. Journal XXII No.3

Leask H.G., St. Mochta's House Louth, Louth Arch. & Hist. Journal IX No.1 & XI I

McGuinness Marie -Project Leader, Carlingford Lough: A Cross Border Youth Study, R & S Printers, Monaghan 1988

McNeill Charles & Rutven-Otway A.J., Dowdall Deeds, Irish Manuscripts Commission 1960

McQuillan Jack, The Railway Town, Dundalgan Press 1993

Mitchell Frank, The Irish Landscape, Collins 1976

Mitchell Frank, Rockmarshall Kitchen Middens, Louth Arch. & Hist. Journal XI,3 & XII,I

Mitchell Frank, "Elk" Skull Newtownbabe, Louth Arch. & Hist. Journal X No.2

Murray L.P., Danish Louth, Louth Arch. & Hist. Journal II No.I

Murray L.P., Ancient Territories, Oirghialla, Uladh, Connaille, Louth Arch. & Hist. Journal III No.3

Murray L.P., Omeath, Comprehensive Survey, Louth Arch. & Hist. Journal III No.3

Nolan J. & Baily W.H., Memoirs of the Geological Survey Sheet 70, HMSO 1877

O'Sullivan Harold, The Franciscans in Dundalk, Seanchas Ardmhacha 4. No.1

O'Sullivan Harold, Jacobite Ascendancy and Williamite Revolution, Louth Arch. & Hist. Journal XXII No.4

O'Sullivan Harold, Eighteenth Century Maps Clanbrassil Estate Dundalk, Louth Arch. & Hist. Journal XV No.1

O'Sullivan Harold, 1575 Rent-roll and Maps Bagenal Estate Carlingford, Louth Arch. & Hist. Journal XXI No.1

O'Sullivan Harold, Cromwellian and Restoration Settlements Dundalk, Louth Arch. & Hist. Journal XIX No.1

Smith Brendan, The Bruce Invasion and County Louth 1315 to 1318, Louth Arch. & Hist. Journal XXII No.1

Tempest H.G., Gossiping Guide to Dundalk and County Louth, Old Dundalk Society/Dundalgan Press 1983

Ua Dubhthaigh Padraic, The Book of Dundalk, Dundalk 1946

Ulster Society for Medieval Latin (ed), The Life of Saint Monenna by Conchubranus, Seanchas Ardmhacha 9 No.1, 10 No 1 & 2

Walsh Katherine, A Fourteenth Century Primate Richard Fitzralph, Clarendon Press 1981

Whittow J.B., Geology and Scenery in Ireland, Penguin Books 1974.

Local directory and sponsors

Cottage Publications would like to express their sincere thanks to the following businesses and organisations without whose help and support this book would not have been possible.

NAME AND ADDRESS	TEL	FAX
Artist		
Gerry Clarke, Drumbilla, Kilcurry	042 77620	
Auctioneering		
P. B. Gunne Ltd, 18 Clanbrassil Street, Dundalk	042 35066	042 34642
Bank		
AIB Bank, Clanbrassil Street, Dundalk	042 31168	042 35775
Bookshop & Book Sourcing Service		
Carroll's Bookshops:		
Dundalk Shopping Centre (Angela)	042 33719	042 31663
The Long-walk Centre (Brian)	042 27283	042 36989
Brewing/Bottling/Canning Beer		
Guinness Ireland Group Ltd, Dundalk Packaging, Ardee Road, Dundalk	042 35441	042 26510
China, Crystal & Gifts		
R. Q. O'Neill, Earl Street, Dundalk	042 34718	042 33832
Coal Merchants		
Bord Na Móna, T/A CCO, The Quays, Dundalk	042 35461	042 39064
County Council		
Louth County Council, Court House, Crowe Street, Dundalk	042 35457	042 34549
Crafts		
Tholsel Crafts, Ghan Cottage, Carlingford	042 73363	

Name and address		Tel	Fax
Decorative Arts in Glass			
Frances' Studio Ltd, Bolies, Castlebellingham		042 72279	042 72749
Delicatessan			
Connolly's Delicatessan, Dundalk Shopping Centre		042 33711/34360	042 32068
Department Stores			
McEvoys Department Stores	Clanbrassil Street, Dundalk	042 33030	042 27919
	West Street, Drogheda	041 37380	
Domestic Refuse Collection & Skip Hire			
Faulkner's, Castlebellingham		042 72258	
Electronics Control Systems			
TSM Control Systems, Demesne Road, Dundalk		042 35560	042 34422
e-mail – tsmcont@iol.ie			
Web site address – www.ie.euro-tradelink.com/tsm.htm			
Food Market			
Smyth's Centra, Tallanstown		042 74291	042 74291
Fresh Produce Import & Distribution			
Fyffes Group Ireland Ltd, The Ramparts, Dundalk		042 35451	042 31685
General Merchants, Fertilisers & Wedding Gifts			
P. Lavelle & Son's Ltd, 80 New Road, Tullydonnell, Silverbridge		(08) 01693 888216	
Historical Research			
Harold O'Sullivan, 9 Dowdallshill, Dundalk		042 34863	
Hotel			
McKevitts' Village Hotel, Market Square, Carlingford		042 73116	042 73144

NAME AND ADDRESS	TEL	FAX
Hotels & Leisure Centre		
Fairways Hotel & Leisure Centre, Dublin Road, Dundalk	042 21500	042 21511
Interior Construction		
Ardmac Group Ltd, Coes Road, Dundalk	042 36711	042 31681
Local Authority		
Dundalk Urban District Council, Town Hall, Dundalk	042 32276	042 36761
Lounge Bar & Restaurant		
The Lisdoo Arms, Newry Road, Dundalk	042 34829	
Oil Distributors		
Four Counties Oil Co. Ltd, Newry Road, Dundalk	042 32299	042 35288
Picture Framers		
Picture Framers & Art Suppliers Ltd, 55 Dublin Road, Dundalk	042 34534	042 34534
Post Office, Convenience Store & Coal Merchants		
Finnegans Foodmarket, Louth Village	042 74101/74185	
Public House		
Daniel McNello & Co, Candlefort, Inniskeen	042 78355	
Restaurant		
The Oyster Catcher, Market Square, Carlingford	042 73922	
Trophies & Corporate Incentives		
Trend Trophies Ltd, Bridge-A-Crinn, Dundalk	042 77151	042 77406
Weather Seals		
Exitex, Mountpleasant, Dundalk	042 71244	042 71221

Dear Reader

We hope you have found this book both enjoyable and useful. This is just one of our range of illustrated titles. Other areas currently featured include:–

Strangford Shores
The Mournes
Armagh

Also available in our "Illustrated History & Companion Range" are:

Ballycastle and the Heart of the Glens
Larne and the Road to the Glens
Coleraine and the Causeway Coast
Bangor
Ballymoney
Lisburn
Newtownards.

Ballymena,
Banbridge,
City of Derry,
Hillsborough
Holywood,
Newry

The paintings featured in each of the titles are also available as signed artists prints.

If you require any further information please call or fax us on (01247) 883876,
E-Mail us on cottage_publ@online.rednet.co.uk
or write to:–

Cottage Publications
15 Ballyhay Road
Donaghadee, Co. Down
N. Ireland, BT21 0NG